THE DEBAUCHER

THE DEBAUCHER

POEMS

Jason Camlot

Copyright © 2008 Jason Camlot

All rights reserved. No part of this publication may be reproduced, stored in a retrieval system or transmitted, in any form or by any means, without the prior written permission of the publisher or, in case of photocopying or other reprographic copying, a license from Access Copyright, 1 Yonge Street, Suite 1900, Toronto, Ontario, Canada, M5E 1E5.

Library and Archives Canada Cataloguing in Publication

Camlot, Jason, 1967-
    The debaucher / Jason Camlot.

Poems.
ISBN 978-1-897178-61-4

    I. Title.

PS8555.A5238D42 2008   C811'.6   C2008-901010-8

The publisher gratefully acknowledges the support of the Canada Council, the Ontario Arts Council and the Department of Canadian Heritage through the Book Publishing Industry Development Program.

Printed and bound in Canada

Insomniac Press
192 Spadina Avenue, Suite 403
Toronto, Ontario, Canada, M5T 2C2
www.insomniacpress.com

For Cory

*I am not a dirty old man, my love
O I am not at all what men say I am*
　　—Irving Layton

*We were not born
to linger around the world so long, making art.*
　　—Robert Allen

Table of Contents

The Debaucher	13
Aphids	25
Côte St. Luc	27
Debaucher's Epigram for Muses	30
The Slave	31
American Culture Association: Boston, 2007	33
Inspiration	34
Gazette 30/04/07 (a day on which nothing of consequence happened to the people I love)	40
Petition to Be Entombed at St. Viateur Bagel	41
Debaucher's Wake-Up Call	45
Lie-Lover	46
To Your Pink	47
The Lake Mussels	48
Since I have stuck my tongue…	49
The Spades	50
Shampoo	51
Big Wheel	52
Mouse Memorial	53
Debaucher's Chivalric Epic-gram	54
Orlando at the Moat	55
Oliver Shards	63
The Death of Roland As Peanuts Panels	64
Angerous Erritory	69
Debaucher Trivia	70

ADIOS SONNETS 71

Saddle Blanket Sonnet 73
Kaos 74
Strudels 75
Hutchison 76
Sonnet of the Bars 77
Summer Caravan 78
Adiós Sonnet 79
Trilby 80
Les Méchants Mardis 81
Inscriptions 82
Sonnet of A to H 83
Sonnet of J to Z 84
Showdown 85
News 86
Sonnet after Daniil Kharms 87
Sunday 88
Times 89
Satellite Sonnet 90
Fable 91
Petersburg 92
Atwater Market 93
Sonnet of the 7th Moon 94
Owls 95
At the OK 96
Epigram 97
After Antigone 98
Lines for a White Cat 99
Variation on "Making It" 100
Sonnet after Valéry 101
Sonnet after Verlaine 102

Sonnet after Baudelaire	103
House Party	104
Advice on Angry Mourning	105
Road Trip	106
Write, Drink, Sleep, Dream	107
Aube Lumière	108
Cliff House Blues	109
I am writing just because I can	110
Acknowledgments	112

The Debaucher

1.

Who is the debaucher?
He is not a bad man.
He is, I'm sure, pure
with wild intention.
He is, as they say,
the "childish roué…
with a burning purity"
to lead you astray.
He means no harm
to those in whom he must
incite a change of course
for better or for worse.
He is the inkling in you,
little red devil
near your left ear,
suggesting casually
that it might not be such a bad thing
if you were to stay, maybe,
an hour or two more,
just to see what will occur.
It might be very interesting,
you can hear him whispering.
How can you not delay
your return home,
when things may be
in the process of evolving
into something

potentially life altering?
The debaucher understands
each moment is just once.
His understanding is chronic.
He feels what's imminent
as ceaseless, painful breathing
(only it is pleasurable for him)
and he is compelled
to remind you because, well,
you are prone to forget
that time moves,
that time moves
and you are not really
alive at all
if you do not move, too,
in some direction
you had not expected.

2.

Débaucher is traditionally a verb.
It might have meant to un-bench
(de-*bauche*) someone, that is, to disturb
him in his work, to wrench
him from the shop
and lead him to the alley
or the bar. It's French.
Desbauch, debosh, debaush, deboach, debauch.
It used to rhyme with *approach*
but now it rhymes with *botch*.
While not related
to *Déboucher* or *Déboucheur*
meaning, metaphorically,
to unmouth and mouth opener,
but more literally, to uncork
and bottle opener,
there are similarities: both work
to make things flow
in new directions,
both words come from French.
It makes me think of a sonnet
Rob wrote, "Sonnet:
Rimbaud Made Me Do It."
Rimbaud and Baudelaire and Mallarmé
made him into the poet that he was.
They trespassed the order of his daily
surroundings, and painful translations
brought him pleasurable revelations.
He tried in his naiveté to be

as daring and intensely bodily,
and visionary, as they were,
as he could be, still living
in the suburbs.
We cannot do in English
what they do in French.
And when we try,
it ends up sounding very dirty.
So, there's a brief etymology.

3.

The debaucher is not necessarily
a person. It can be a memory,
or the absence of compelling
memory, or deliberately selective
memory. It can be fear,
because fear keeps us from choosing
certain paths, and consequently chooses other paths.
It can be sudden love.
It can be a sense of right and good,
or a diverting taste of blood.
It can jam us like a broken cash machine.
It can be an act of sound, like rhyme.
Rhyme makes poetry debauch.
It leads a line regrettably astray.
It jars us off into apposite thought.
With sound, rhyme makes things touch that shouldn't touch.
Caresses move from hand to knee to crotch
O so quickly when rhyme's allowed its way.
And then everything changes instantly.
Adjacent thoughts that had been friendly and pragmatic,
now set aflame by rhyme, become dramatic.
A rhyme can give a word radical new meaning.
When Byron rhymes *bottle* with *Aristotle*,
it makes me want to drink metaphysics
ice cold, on a hot day, without a glass.
It makes me want to drink beer until I'm sick,
I mean really puking so it's coming out of me like
    liquefied petroleum gas,
like those undergrads up in Montreal for the weekend from U Mass

(those guys are friggin' hilarious)
who drink until they pass out on the grass,
next day wake up with shards of beer bottle glass
stuck in their ass
and then lament, *Alas,*
I may have to miss Monday morning chemistry class,
and then my chemistry teacher will lambaste
me in front of my peers when I come back,
because that guy loves to sass
us about how we don't care to unlock the secrets of matter and mass,
but just want to fumble with the clasps
of drunken girls' bra straps.
O God, please let me pass
my final exam, the last
chemistry test I'll ever have to pass,
because I'm switching into modern languages,
because I'm really strong at "Compare and Contrast."
O God, please let there be a question about the molecular breakdown of
   liquefied petroleum gas.

4.

More commonly we think of him
As the depraved wooer
Who takes a woman from her rightful home
To fondle her and screw her.

James Harris, in the famous ballad,
Is an excellent specimen
Of a debaucher who woos a woman away
From her husband and children.

James Harris was the original love
Of the well-born damsel Jane Reynolds.
He returns to her after seven years,
Entices her with ships of gold.

There are eight versions of this song
In Child's anthology of ballads;
It's only clear in a few versions
That James Harris is intrinsically bad.

Of course, one such version (243E)
Is the most popular one today;
She's lovely when she spies his cloven foot
After he's sailed her out to sea.

It's easy for us when James Harris
Is so obviously the devil;
We love to know the debaucher's bad
And that corruption is evil.

But, even in this straightforward version,
Jane Reynolds is given something of her own.
The Daemon gives her a final gift
Before he brings her down.

Before he sinks the ship in a flash of fire
To the bottom of the sea,
The Daemon Lover takes Jane to the topmast high
To see what she could see.

I hope when I die I'll be raised up high
So that I can look around,
And see all the people I love
Still living on the ground.

5.

Maybe he's with me, but how can I know?
If, when you are forty years old,
attempting to finish
a poem about being led astray,
and you get a call from your childhood friend
who's ditching work
to go for lunch.
And you leave the poem
off halfway
through, to have a Wilensky's
Light Lunch Special,
and then another very old friend
shows up, so you have a Top
and second cherry soda,
while he eats *his* Special,
and then your two friends
ask what you're doing
with the rest of the day,
and it's the first truly
hot afternoon of spring,
so hot it feels like the dead
of summer, and somehow you find
yourself back at your first friend's house,
downloading guitar tabs
to ABBA and Avril Lavigne songs
so you can sing them
over and over again,
piano, guitar and three voices,
well into the evening,

and you find yourself,
perhaps past middle age,
singing "St. James Infirmary,"
one piano, one voice,
well into the night.
If, at dawn, you find yourself
alone, with hoarse voice
and sore fingertips,
too drunk and stoned
to care that you have
ashes in your hair,
that you have lost one sandal,
that you have lost your glasses,
your car keys,
your discretion.
If, as dawn is breaking
in the city's sky,
you find yourself there
at the corner gas station
eating Heavenly Hash ice cream
from a tub, with your hands.
If, about halfway through
the tub of delicious ice cream,
your cell phone rings,
and you answer
with ice cream hands
and it is your wife,
who has been up already
forty-five minutes,
because it's 7 a.m. now
and she's preparing for work,

and she asks, straightforwardly,
because she's truly curious,
she asks through the cell phone,
Where are you?
And you reply,
I'm just around the corner, baby,
at the gas station
around the corner.
I'm just eating some ice cream.
And then there is silence, of course,
because that's what makes
a cell phone feel, at this hour,
like a sonnet,
an unrequited, unanswered
sonnet, excised from its series,
as you press your cheek
to its compact rows
of green-lit number buttons,
and implore to your love,
I'm just eating ice cream, baby.
I'll be home real soon, baby.
Perfect love sonnet silence
amplified by carbon filaments,
micro-tele-cell-sonnet phone
technology, that makes us feel
exactly where we are.
I'll be home real soon, baby.
If you find yourself
closing your ice cream—
covered cell phone,
slipping it in your front pocket

and digging in deep to finish off
the tub before you
walk the two blocks home,
then, in all likelihood,
the debaucher has come
to you, as a quiet voice,
or as a vision, or a feeling
of life,
of love for life.
In all likelihood,
the debaucher has called
numerous times
within the last 24 hours.
Say a prayer of thanks.
The debaucher has come.

Aphids

The worst mistake in life or literature is to have the wrong feeling.
　—Louis Dudek

There are no real swans, only imaginary ones.
But imaginary swans still suffer.

Life is short and art long, unless you outlive yourself.
In that instance, you have your whole life to mourn in art.

Axioms are not axioms unless the letter x is available.
But for how long can we rely upon the letter x?

When you say, "I'm sorry," I don't want to look at you.
But then I can't see if I still please you.

Absence makes the heart bleed profusely.
The heart loves to swim in blood and absinthe.

If I love you, I am not telling you.
If you ask, I will have to kill you.

Men and women are the only animals that blush.
And some fish sometimes deign to blush.

Aphids have piercing-sucking mouthparts called stylets.
See tiny Aphrodite in her sharp *styletto* heels.

Beware of the man who abides by only one book.
But if he loses it, help him find his one book.

A cigarette is a perfect kind of love. Ashes are a perfect form of death.
An ashtray is like dying in a drained Motel 8 Jacuzzi.

Lies are only bad if they cause pain, truths are always good.
Truths can cause severe pain, but they are still right.

The superfluous can be most useful to someone.
Go to the superfluous store to find just what you need.

Aphorisms should be distinguished from axioms.
But who has the time, what with maxims and proverbs and whatnot.

The worst mistake in life or literature is to have the wrong feeling.
Come to me and I will tell you which of your feelings is wrong.

Côte St. Luc

אַן מכּליך אװ דזאָסט אָט גועלף ראָד
סיד פּעלם בײסמענט װי אַר דוינג אָר אָד

On McAlear Ave., just off Guelph Rd.,
Syd Pell's basement, we're doing our ode

to the Beatles, "Back in the USSR"
into "Come Together" into "Get Back" and then the Cars,

"Just What I Needed" and then "Jumpin'
Jack Flash" and "Paint It, Black" lumped in

at the end, even though we don't know all the chords.
It doesn't matter because we know all the words,

even the "black as gold" line during the tail-end
fade-out part. I'm learning how to bend

the notes in the solo to "Another Brick
in the Wall, Part 2," to edge my guitar pick

against the strings and get that harmonic ring.
I play the intro to Hendrix's "Little Wing"

not too badly, as Syd sits on two green Sealtest
milk crates (his drum stool) and tests

his foot speed on the black Ludwig kick drum,
muffled with a frayed old needlepoint cushion.

Then lunch is over, it's time to get back
to school, wolf down the fries we asked

the boys to pick up for us at Delly Boys
(Corner Westminster and Côte St. Luc Rd.), make noise

in the halls on the way to Miss Caiserman's Yiddish class,
develop better, more ridiculous ways to harass

this poor, kind, yet frighteningly bipolar teacher,
invent new devices with which to make our missiles reach her.

There's no truly dark sarcasm in our classroom.
Just lines like, "Hey! Kids! Leave those teachers on lithium
    alone!"

It's a warm spring day in Côte St. Luc, the windows
are all open. Already, Passover and Yom Hashoah

are behind us, the harvest holiday, Shavuot,
is still to come. Our hearts are beating faster by the minute

just because we are fifteen, and it's a warm spring day.
Our lives are as unserious as our high school names:

J, Syd, Bri, Dave, Mini, Phil Rez,
Giggy, Piggy, Tordj, Jeff ("He Knows") Moness....

Miss Klein, niece of Abraham Moses, is our guidance counsellor.
And not far, somewhere off Kildare, lives another daring dikhter
(poet).

In twenty-five years or so, they will create *avenue Irving Layton*,
A quiet street near Guelph Rd. and Parkhaven,

nine blocks from where we wrote exams,
smoked up, judged and loved each other, held epic lunchtime jams.

Debaucher's Epigram for Muses

Missed the dead things at the museum.
Had to go see about a carpe diem.

The Slave

Mixed Media: Floor, Walls, Cassock Daughter.

In this art installation, you are a pious Jew captured by cassocks, transported a slave into this conceptual art piece. The room is seventeenth-century Polish peasant, with a wooden floor and simple utensils for eating and straw for sleeping. When you are not transporting water or mending leather, you reside in this room and attempt to remember. First you are occasionally distracted from your remembering by Wanda, your master's vulgar daughter. She comes to you with a desire to learn about your superior system of morals, and with thick, healthy haunches. As the years pass, everything you once knew is carved into your floor. And as more years pass, these carved letters appear to you as meaningless scratches. Then, your memory of God falls in inverse proportion to the rise of your desire for Wanda. Ah, Wanda. She is the bright spot in this installation. She is so primitive and good. She sees you as a delicate, civilized man, even as you, after eighteen years in captivity, away from books, rabbinical argument and study, would be just a pitiful retard among your own people. A shmegege (shmeg•geh'•geh). As Wanda writhes on top of you, seeking deeply into your dark eyes for approval that she is something more than a barbarian, you cannot stop repeating in your head, "I-am-a-shme-geh-geh. I-am-a-shme-geh-geh. I-am-a-shme-geh-geh…" As time goes on, you forget even the meaning of the word, shmegege (an idler, buffoon, idiot, fool). Yet despite having forgotten everything that had made you, once, a pious Jew, you can never see Wanda as anything but a wretched animal.

American Culture Association: Boston, 2007

After hearing sign-up poets in a hotel meeting room,
One feels the need to cultivate a list of *noms de plume:*

Hart Crap, Wallace Stupid, William Carlos Won't,
H. De-formed, Elizabeth Dipshit, Sylvia Death, Anne Sexy-not.

All the Fens drinking dens have been flattened by flat screens,
Tiki bars killed by style bars, soon the Monster won't be Green.

The Rat is dead, Deli Haus dead, Nuggets barely found,
Kenmore Square is gone, Banana Republicked to the ground.

So taxi your way to Allston, take a stroll up Harvard Ave.,
See frosh transporting two-fours like rows of horny, drunken elves.

Get carded by a twelve-year-old at Harper's Ferry Bar,
Scream threats at louts on grassy knolls in Stanley Ringer Park.

Sing a song to Blanchard's Liquors, it's a song you've sung before,
That's Blanchard's, 103 Harvard Ave., Allston, MA, 02134.

Inspiration

Mixed Media: Poet, Cannibals, Banquet Table with Fittings, Candlelight

In this installation, two cannibals are supping on the poet artie gold. You are sitting at the delicately set banquet table upon which the poet artie gold is served. You are seated across from the two cannibals. You watch and listen as they make their progress through the poet.

Cannibal 1: Look, there are two tomcats in here.

Cannibal 2: Remarkable. How do you imagine they got there?

Cannibal 1: How can they possibly fit?

Cannibal 2: One tomcat for each of us. (They eat the tomcats of artie gold, quietly. After a while, the cannibals engage in conversation again.)

Cannibal 1: Do you want this Jack Spicer?

Cannibal 2: No. You go ahead. (Pause.) But I would like to have *extra* Frank O'Hara, if you are going to eat all the Spicer.

Cannibal 1: Fine. I'll just finish my O'Hara, first. (Cannibal 1 now talking with his mouth full.) What's your favourite line from an artie gold poem?

Cannibal 2: Would you mind not talking while you chew? I like Frank O'Hara, but I'd prefer not to see him like that in your mouth. (Cannibal 1 swallows.)

Cannibal 1: I apologize.

Cannibal 2: He looked orange in your mouth. It was quite disgusting.

Cannibal 1: I said I'm sorry.

Cannibal 2: Fine.

Cannibal 1: So?

Cannibal 2: Right, favourite line from an artie gold poem. (Pause.) I guess it would have to be either, "in this package of skin," or that part in the poem titled "Frank O'Hara" where he refers to "deadly parties// where the voices/ were tinged with vodkas/ coloured/ with bright syrups."

Cannibal 1: Good choices. (Pause.) Shall we eat the voice now?

Cannibal 2: Fine idea. Let's split it down the middle, lengthwise, so we each get a taste of every tone.

Cannibal 1: Fine idea. (They eat artie gold's voice for a while.)

Cannibal 2: Aren't you going to ask me what *my* favourite line from an artie gold poem is?

Cannibal 1: Okay, shoot. What's your favourite line from an artie gold poem?

Cannibal 2: Well, there are so many.

Cannibal 1: Okay. But if you had to choose *one*.

Cannibal 2: Well, since you ask, I'd say it must be…it's probably…I'd say it's "Scottish" from that poem "Five for Bruce."

Cannibal 1: "Scottish"?

Cannibal 2: Yes, definitely. "Scottish" from the poem, "Five for Bruce" in his book *Even yr photograph looks afraid of me.*

Cannibal 1: But "Scottish" isn't a line. It's just a word.

Cannibal 2: But it inhabits a line unto itself in that poem.

Cannibal 1: Granted, but it hardly makes sense as a "favourite" cited out of context like that. Out of the context of the poem, it's just the word *Scottish*.

Cannibal 2: Not for me, it isn't.

Cannibal 1: Would you mind passing the nouns, please?

Cannibal 2: Certainly. (Cannibal 2 passes artie gold's nouns to Cannibal 1. They share in the nouns for a while.)

Cannibal 1 (Continuing his train of thought): I mean, the opening of that poem "The Relativity of Spring"—"The nouns are hungry for sense/ The facts are not known/ They are tasteless by which is meant/ They are hard to transcribe/ They taste the colour of the sky against cement"—now that's what I mean when I say "favourite line."

Cannibal 2: That was more like a passage, than a line. Can you pass the facts, please?

Cannibal 1: Certainly.

Cannibal 2: Thank you. (They eat artie gold's facts.)

Cannibal 1: Fine. Have it your way. What's your favourite *passage* from an artie gold poem?

Cannibal 2: Well, that would probably have to be the passage from one of the untitled ones where he imagines people who had nightmares, "nightmares our bodies older than the ancientest sea tortoise/ blue in detroit aquariums that slowly cruised into surgery/ where artists laboured into the small morning hours…" etcetera. I like the idea of an artist working as a surgeon on a body that has been turned into the oldest sea tortoise.

Cannibal 1: That *is* a good passage.

Cannibal 2: Don't you think tortoise is more delicious when pronounced with French accentuation, so that it rhymes with *because*?

Cannibal 1: *Tortoise*. Yes, I agree. artie gold's tortoise *is* more delicious when I pronounce it that way. (They eat artie gold's *tortoise* for a while.)

Cannibal 2: Can you finish artie gold's asthma?

Cannibal 1: I can't finish it. Can you?

Cannibal 2: No, I can't finish it.

Cannibals 1 & 2 (Looking directly at you, the museum patron, now): Can *you* finish artie gold's asthma?

Gazette 30/04/07 (a day on which nothing of consequence happened to the people I love)

City paves the way to dark repairs.
Cops swarm the streets with six potholes fewer.

The Reds back JT for a déjà vu.
Humiliation sounds in interview.

Tae-kwon-do officials ban hijabs.
St. James United Church breaks out in jazz.

Marchers join world protests vs. bloodbath.
Teen drivers flee the fuzz in minivans.

New dangers are revealed for conjoined twins.
Ministers repent to welfare recipients.

A hostage drama ends in Chilliwack.
"Autonomy" is floated by the Bloc.

Terrorist strikes rise 29%.
Iran will attend the Iraq summit.

Cellphones are used to "escape" jail cells.
Asian companies show great potential.

Mackenzie Growth's on track for a strong year.
Elbonians labour the night, making sneakers.

The Honda CR-V EX finishes first.
C.S.L. 5 ½ avail. immed. or July 1st.

Petition to Be Entombed at St. Viateur Bagel

To the tune of "Supplique pour être enterré sur une plage de Sète" by George Brassens.

Death Allegorical, who's never forgiven me
For stuffing weed in holes where his eyes used to be,
Is wheezing (metaphorically) down my neck.
Cornered as I am by freshly raked burial plots,
It seems time to update my last will and testament,
To write a final tombstone cheque.

Dipped in the toxic green ink of the St. Lawrence,
Dipped in wading pools of suburban ignorance,
And guided by a shaky hand,
Good Bic, record what to do with my dead body
Once life and art have grown terminally bored of me,
Scribble a few simple demands:

When my soul flies east down the Metropolitan
Towards those of Leonard Cohen and Oscar Peterson,
Aldo Nova and Corey Hart,
Get my corpse a seat at the back of the 80 bus
(use the transfer attached herein for this purpose),
Send it down L'avenue du Parc.

To quote Uncle Mort, "We don't have our own 'watering hole.'
We're some at de la Savane, some lie in D.D.O.
Sure, Mount Royal Cemetery would be a thrill.
But why spend that kind of cash on yourself when you're dead,
When you can blow it at the Casino instead?"
No family yearnings to fulfill.

Two blocks from Olympico, across from where Zorba's was
(Zorba's, where I once composed "Mr. Fedora"):
B A E L and a big G
On the middle window of the storefront triptych,
Glass fogged by wet boots and heat from the oven bricks,
Sidewalk sprinkled with sesame seeds.

Next door a barber shaved me raw on my wedding day—
I lived on St. Urbain, my bride lived on Waverly—
Monday floor hockey at the Y.
Evenings with my guitar on the back balcony,
One block from everyone I'd ever want to see,
Where else would I want to die?

Sure, there are other spots that would be nearly as good,
Like under my '65 Rambler's colossal hood,
Afloat in the Julep's giant sphere,
Or in old apartments on Du Rocher, Dorion,
Mount-Royal, Coloniale, Casgrain, Du Bullion—
But no place compares to here.

Swinging on wooden swings in green Kindersley Park,
Smoking a joint and swinging alone after dark,
I wondered what I would become.
A pastoral atmosphere is fine for imagining
How I might, sometime soon, go somewhere, do something,
Vaguely, how I might become someone.

More concretely, I climbed crab apple tree branches,
Felt, through Jordache jeans, young girls' haunches and crotches,
In satin blouses I found teenage love.
I learned that some girls are more playful than others,
Some have older sisters, some have younger brothers,
Some hands are hard to let go of.

With all due respect and honour to Leonard Cohen
(from me, a belated troubadour, epigone),
May Our Man of Song forgive me.
For though his grave will be more trumpeted, glorious,
Deep, better visited, flowered, uproarious—
Mine will be way more seedy.

This tomb, sandwiched between the oven and the cash,
Won't depress customers who come in for a *nosh*.
They'll hardly know it's there at all.
Built out of freezer doors ruined in the last ice storm,
People will think it's a locker for bagel crumbs, or
A diminutive bathroom stall.

Is it too much to ask: on my little burial plot,
Stick up pictures and notes from my friends, with fridge magnet
Flattering things, if possible.
Omit evidence of my life's great concessions,
And photos of my most embarrassing life lessons.
Make it seem like my life was full.

Then, when tourists come all the way from Burlington,
Plattsburgh and Ottawa, Oshawa and Verdun,
Addis Ababa and Peking,
They'll discover a neighbourhood poet who died,
Have something to ponder while they wait, and divide,
"Eight sesame, four poppy seed."

And, when at 4 a.m. a seventeen-year-old
Comes in for shelter from his blank peers, and the cold,
And reads a snippet from a poem
That I wrote when I was not much older than him,
The closing couplet of a teenage battle hymn,
Bread and poetry will keep him warm.

Something I wrote when I was not much older than him,
The closing couplet of a teenage battle hymn:
Step through these doors, shut out the storm.
Bread and poetry will keep you warm.

Debaucher's Wake-Up Call

I dream until my tiny warning bells
Alert me to drab heavens, ho-hum hells.

Lie-Lover

When I see you in the frozen food aisle,
searching lazily to music that pours
from the ceiling, with your American Apparel eyes,
and with chromatic scales of green on your fore-
head, from florescent lights and linoleum floors
emitting and reflecting via tubes and tiles
the pale, greenish-white found in cucumbers,
I think, "With such perfectly ripened thighs,
she'll need to be bitten into with a smile."
How beautiful you are, and shallower
than the tide pools of a Safeway lobster.
So what? Who seeks "high fibre" from sugar pie,
laments "no pit" in a maraschino cherry?

After Baudelaire's "L'Amour du mensonge"

To Your Pink

Your pink dress pleases me. The way it clings
to your tits, juts your throat, shows off your pits,
and coats you like a swarm of wet bee wings,
bee wings from wet pink bees. It really fits

you well, this satin dress. Where'd you get it?
Did you shed it, like a pink snake, in your sleep,
find it on the floor, decide to slip it
on this evening to make sure I'd want to peel

it off you again tonight? Where'd this pink
come from: flowers, nipples, Venus's plate?
Or did it arise like a blush in your cheeks,
and then whelm your figure, just to desecrate

the modesty that tinted it? I doubt,
actually, your pink is that devout.

After Théophile Gautier's "À une robe rose"

The Lake Mussels

Listen, lake. I'm talking to you. Listen
rocks and caves. Listen, dark forests.
It's stupid, but I need you to listen
to me carefully, now. I was obsessed

with the barmaid from Mussel's Cocktail Lounge,
and you were here when I persuaded her
to join me in this boat, drink beer, go down
on me, as we floated beneath a blur

of summer stars. I hope you're listening, stars.
You were all here as she and I scraped our
knees on the row boat's wet, sand-crusted floor,
as we banged aluminium, dislodged an oar

from its oarlock socket. Listen, dark cove.
Your mollusk-tang is hard to get rid of!

After Alphonse de Lamartine's "Le lac"

Since I have stuck my tongue...

Since I have stuck my tongue in your wet cup,
since I have felt my head between your hands,
since I have sniffed the perfume of your glands,
released into your bloodstream, out your duct,

since I have sniffed the sweet breath of your soul,
since I have sought it, buried in shadows,
since I have loved you as Vincent van Gogh
yearned to love that "model," Rachel, with his whole

being, so much so he put his own ear
into her hand and said, "Keep this object
carefully." Since I know you don't object
to engaging in nightly, oral prayer,

I can tell Time, with his dire ashen cup,
what to do with it, where to shove it up.

After Victor Hugo's "Puisque j'ai mis ma lèvre"

The Spades

Le gel durcit les eaux...

Street puddles harden;
souvlaki-joint windows whiten with frost.

To the east on St. Catherine girls invade
the Burger King, or scuttle in rhinestone
heels like catwalk models in an air raid
toward *dépanneurs*, or into taxis home.

Wads of filthy, frozen gum look like dead
toads on the street, plastic straws like striped reeds
rolling under cars. A slow kick drum beats
heavily for a moment, then recedes.

Now the clubs are closed. Vacuum *camionettes*
suck up waste through huge, corrugated snouts.
A shirtless Hoosick (NY) frosh scrambles a deck
of playing cards reduced to just one suit.

No clubs, diamonds, no hearts, just trembling spades
floating the street. An ominous parade.

After Émile Verhaeren's "La bêche"

Shampoo

Summer social slow dance, we were twelve,
your pants were satin, my white jeans were swelled,
swollen, from dancing slowly, and from your smell,
Clairol shampoo, clear Cherry-Doo hair gel,

plus the salty neck buried beneath your hair.
I was happy just to sneak my hand in there,
my nose, and travel to Asia Minor,
hot Africa. Your hair as thick as Cher's

or Crystal Gayle's, a tent of shadows stretched
over my sense of what to do. Impressed
by my knowledge of the lyrics to Zep
songs, you stood us still. My timid hand crept

down your satiny coco, musky back.
Hearts raced like Fonz and Pinky run amok.

After Baudelaire's "La chevelure"

Big Wheel

There's nothing left of that red wine
we drank from coffee mugs that time
we stayed up until five,
when you were alive.

On Monday mornings when I drive
my little bees to their beehive,
I find myself surprised,
then it subsides.

Keep on singing Valentine songs
when you feel alone.
Keep on pondering the sky,
and we will sing along.

When it's dark, the stars sometimes
shine like they have a real design
to signal something fine,
they seem to be trying

to say, "Just run away with all
the people you love,
and place it all on the big wheel,
until you've had enough."

Mouse Memorial

I live with mice inside a monument of mice.
They have lived here since before the First Crusade.
I have been here since I learned to talk.
The mice are proud
and one day I will be a mouse, too—
small, blind and unimportant.
I admire their irreverent creeping, timid squeaks, tiny
ebony nests where their young lie like peanuts.
I admire their precious breath
and fast-beating hearts.
The monument itself is in the fragile bones
of those mice who are still alive.
As human castles lose their walls,
as tinted towers rise and fall,
this scuttling monument endures below,
passed on from mouse parent to mouse child.
My big, awkward bones
are my impediment to being memorial.
Still, already I am unimportant, and I am blind.
Is it hubris to hope one day I will be small?

Debaucher's Chivalric Epic-gram

What do you get when history meets epic?
Meatbone stew and a wounded pipick.

Orlando at the Moat

He came to the moat, and he couldn't cross over,
He couldn't dive in, and he couldn't fly over,
He just stood on the grass, amidst nettles and clover,
Vulnerable to arrows and hot oil, and moreover,
He shed his protective armour, didn't seek cover
From stinging saltpetre and corrosive sulphur,
But looked at her window, and bellowed up to her:

"You don't really know me; I've come to emboss
My family signet across your big yawning fosse.

But before I do, there are things from my history,
You should know, a posteriori.

I first encountered love as a prosthetic issue.
I learned to capture love inside a tissue.

I came to terms with love as misshapen in some sense.
Then I learned that love always misrepresents

Itself to whatever person encounters it,
That love prefers war wounds and germs to transmit,
And would rather explore you than show you its motives,
Unless love comes to you as an impervious ditz,
In which case you take love for ice cream and banana split it.

In my experience it's good to know both:
Love as self-exploration, love as fluidic and gross.

But seriously, I don't think sex is necessary,
So long as there's love and dessert with a cherry.

I've been told that soft whispering can be apropos,
And I've since learned that romance is very much so.
Does that make any sense? It did once long ago.
Here are the sites of my first *quid pro quos*,
The places I learned how to reap what I sow:

First: in the barbarian fields of Africa.
Second: in some isosceles trees of TriBeCa.

Third: in the space between carpe and diem.
Fourth: in a jar of aloe vera hand cream.

Fifth: in a five-act morality play.
Sixth: on a record by NWA.

Seventh: in a fit of passion and jealousy.
Eighth: in the made-up birthdate on a fake ID.
Ninth: at My Lady's parents' estate in the country.
Tenth: in sex positions where *la* comes before Shangri-.
Eleventh: in fragmenting modern consumer society.
Twelfth: in the latex and lube used to stop HIV.
Thirteenth: in the strict codes of love and propriety.

I once knew a girl who was all 'holier-than-them,'
Her favorite question was, 'What's your problem?'
Geeks were her enemies, bitches her friends,
I said to her, 'Lady, with you its just uss-es and thems,
And you know, I think your divisiveness stems

From an unhappy childhood, and not enough gems
Slapping the curtain at your castle's back end.'"

At this the beautiful castle dame stuck her head out,
Showed her porcelain face, with her lips made a pout,
With her hands was devout, with her eyes displayed doubt,
With her lungs and her mouth and her tongue this did shout:

"Are you a man or a mannerist?"

The Lady continued with a whole bunch of questions,
But Orlando replied to the first, ignoring the rest of them:

"My name is Orlando, or just Lando, for short.
Or Landy, for cute,
Roland at war,
O-man when I cavort.
Renaldo at Court,
Or whatever you want, bend my letters athwart,
Kneed me into croissants, whip me into a torte.
I'm here until you agree to make end of this sport.

And then, truce: empty the tank engine into the caboose.
But if I answer your question, maybe then you'll excuse

My need to be coarse, and the smell of my horse.
While I love to persuade, I would, of course, never coerce.

So listen to my personal *Song of Roland*,
Then beg me to unsheath my Durendal, swollen:

I lived in a house on Mission Dolores
But prior to that I lived in a forest

Of Safeway sale stickers and Jack in the Boxes
In a motel apartment that smelled fatally noxious,

And had wall-to-wall carpets that were so obnoxious
With their brown swirly patterns that the Mexican locksmith

When he came to my place to unstick a bent key
Looked sorry for me, said, 'Man, your carpet's UG-LY!'
I said, 'I know it's disgusting, but the rent's $570,
Which was actually cheap for a safe place to sleep.
It had a full kitchenette, a toilet and sink,
The walls in the bedroom were turquoise and pink,

Plywood to write on, a futon to sleep on,
Patio in the back with dead bushes to pee on.
But the squirrels back there were all like Genghis Khan:
Ruthless, bloodthirsty, ready to lay little paws on

Any intruder who stepped out on the deck,
Aching to dig squirrel teeth into eyes and neck.

The squirrels hurled their bodies against the patio doors,
They hissed through the window, they spat and they swore
Such fowl curses I hadn't heard since the Saracen wars,
So, obviously, I couldn't go out there anymore.

Anon, the patio squirrels were the least of my worries.
I'd be nostalgic for rabid demons little and furry.

Soon a brutal assault from the back of my mouth
Lay me out like a lout on my beige Goodwill couch.
With every swallow and bite I screamed, 'Ouch!'

In truth, far worse things were coming out of my *bouche*.
I had an abscessed, impacted wisdom tooth.

Four of them, actually, my tongue was surrounded
By sheathed ivory falchions. My war horn, Olifant, I
    sounded:

'Dear Mother of Mary! Great Holy [*illegible*]
Christians Rock! Pagan Teeth Suck!'
                                      AOI

After days of Jack Daniel's, I went to the dentist,
I mean a dentist with knives, not some dental hygienist.

Dr. Oliver of Sunnyvale lay me out on my backside,
Stuck a mask on my face so I'd breathe nitrous oxide,

Stuck headphones onto my ears so I could hear Yanni
As he sharpened his blades and began cutting into me.

He slit and he sliced, he slashed and he slew,
He pierced and incised, he gashed and he hewed,
Clove the upper-left most-posterior tooth in two,
Extracted both pieces and bid them adieu.
He was the stoutest warrior of the hands that I ever knew.
Doc Oliver then bravely continued
With his goodly brand onto wisdom tooth number two.

The jabbing and digging and deep excavation
Gave me the urge for expectoration,
But Oliver refused, upped my medication,

And switched me from Yanni to the pan flutes of Zamfir,
Which mixed with the clash of metal and bone in my ears.
I dreamed of my horse, I dreamed of my spear,
I dreamed of the Saracen blood I'd used to draw new frontiers,
I dreamed of my valiant warrior peers
Who fought without fear for so many years,
And continued to fight when their wounds were severe.
I thought of how vicious they were, and sincere.
I dreamed of you, My Lady, of having you near,
Of calling you dear,
Of telling you how sexy you look in whatever you wear,
And then, after two hours prostrate in the dental chair,
I, Roland, shed a tear.

I, Roland, felt I was at death's door
And that from both my ears my brains ran forth.
That's what I felt, but soon the surgery was over,
and, as you can see, I have since recovered.

Dr. Oliver had succeeded in removing all four
Of my wisdom teeth. He said my gums would be sore
For two or three days, but then I wouldn't have any pain anymore.

Either the Dr. was overly optimistic,
Or else he was brutally (but professionally) sadistic.

The next three days I lay in bed.
My cheeks were gunpowder, my tongue was lead,

When I drank Odwalla, I upchucked it,
All I could do was moan and spit,
The future seemed a hopeless pit.

But after three days, like Lazarus I rose
With blood on my cheeks and blood on my clothes,

With a bloody white T-shirt, I left the apartment
To search for a joint in my glove compartment.

I sparked it up and started to feel
A bit less pathetic, a bit more surreal.
Like a zombie, I wandered El Camino Real,
Past the liquor store and the vacant Mountain View strip mall.
At the 7-Eleven, I played Terminator II: Judgment Day Pinball,

Bought a Twinkie, my first solid food in three days,
Played more pinball because I'd won a free game.

Spent the rest of the evening outside Lozano Brushless Car Wash,
Watching the brushless car washers with their chamois cloths
Rub off the mosquitos and locusts that had been squashed

Against silvery grilles and tinted windshields.
I watched them Armor All Naugahyde stearing wheels.
All the dead bugs and shiny automobiles
At Lozano Brushless Car Wash on El Camino Real
Made me think of my sword, my horn and my shield,

Made me analyze carefully what I really feel
About the Real as it exists in relation to the Ideal.

After a week of soft foods, I rediscovered
My strength, and decided that I was done with war,
I wasn't going to fight Charles's battles for him anymore.
Done with decapitations, finished with gore,
Fed up with being a ruthless warrior,
I have decided to focus on being your lover.
So here I am, waiting before
Your uncrossable moat and your barred castle door.

It's true, they removed half my head, and all of my wisdom,
But I still have my balls and an inkling of is-dom.
So, what do you say? Will you help mend my schism,
Accept my devotion, true love, and hot jism?"

Orlando's grand speech was finally over.
He stood on the grass, amidst nettles and clover.
From the stinging saltpetre and corrosive sulphur,
Hot oil, stones and arrows he never sought cover.
He just stared at the window of his potential lover.
But she was no longer there, and she would not answer.
From this silence, Roland could never recover.

Oliver Shards

En la grant presse or i fiert cume ber,
Trenchet cez hanstes e cez escuz buclers,
E piez e poinz e seles e costez...
     —*La Chanson de Roland,* CXLVII, ll. 1966–1969

He has such a bloody and valiant rage.
He digs into his horse, gallops with force.
He shreds bucklers and floral shields to foil.
He snaps and splinters spears into toothpicks.
He gouges gorgets, unravels battle mail.
He pierces through armour to ligament.
He cuts off wrists and shoulders, carves up ribs.
He hacks deep through the backbones of horses.
He dashes eyes from the skulls they were in.
He tears off heads like apples from stems.
He severs spines and breaks necks into halves.
He slices hearts in two and dices bones.
He splits brains through corpora callosa.
He spins corpses on the end of his spear.
He flings dead bodies amidst thousands more.
He wears blood up his arms like evening gloves.
He wields his sword, a solid stick of blood.
He loves his sword and peers and Lord right well.
He sends the souls of enemies to hell.

The Death of Roland As Peanuts Panels

☐☐☐☐

Roland feels death near him.
He climbs a little hill,

attempts to kick a football,

falls backwards,

faints there.

☐☐☐☐

The trees are very tall

and filled with kites.

Four stone mounds glow.

Roland faints.

☐☐☐☐

Roland feels he is lost.
He is transparent, except for his outline.

Before him a gray stone mound.

He strikes with Durendal, his sword.

WHOOSH! THUMP! ZOOM! CLUMP! WUMP!

☐☐☐☐

Roland strikes the glowing mound.

The sword grates

but doesn't break or scrape.

Roland can't stand it.

☐☐☐☐

Count Roland strikes the pitcher's mound
with Durendal, his sword.

He whacks it, smacks it, smites it….

The sword grates loudly, but doesn't bend or break.

He laments his glorious sword, quietly:
"Why can't I have a normal sword like everyone else?"

☐☐☐☐

Roland's death
descends from head to heart.

He moves to a white spot beneath a pine tree.

He admits his wrongs,
He taps his chest with steady little beats.

Roland extends his baseball glove to God.

☐☐☐☐

Roland knows his time is over.

[blank panel]

SIGH

Angels from heaven descend.

☐☐☐☐

Count Roland lay on a white hill
beneath a pine tree.

He turned his face,
remembered his little friends,
lamented them all.

He extended his right-hander's glove to God.

Angel Gabriel took it.

☐☐☐☐

Roland is dead.

[blank panel]

[blank panel]

Now God has his soul.

Translated/adapted from La Chanson de Roland, *Paris, Bordas, 1984, Lines 2259–2397, and* The Complete Peanuts 1957–1958 *&* 1959–1960, *New York: W. W. Norton, 2005 & 2006.*

Angerous Erritory

Artist or atavist?
Beatific or beastialist?
Courteous or carnalist?
Decent or duplicitous?
Earnest or euphuist?
Faithful or fallacious?
Graceful or garrulous?
Hunk or heretic?
Integral or ironist?
Jongleur or journalist?
Knight or katzenjammerist?
Lover or libidinist?
Nice or narcissist?
Open-hearted or odious?
Prince or pleasurist?
Quiet or quarrelist?
Righteous or recidivist?
Sincere or satirist?
True or terrorist?
Upright or undulationist?
Valiant or vandalist?
Worthy or wound with wickedness?
Exemplary or excrement?
Yale Man or Yiddishist?
Zeus or zombified zilchnic?

Debaucher Trivia

What does it matter what you say about people?
What's the last word in *A Touch of Evil*?

Adios Sonnets
For Robert Edward Allen (1946–2006)

Saddle Blanket Sonnet

On your flying saddle blanket today
you were perfectly warm in buffalo skin,
meticulous with numerous fingers,
incredulous, handsome (like Errol Flynn),

peaceful (like a child), stoic, heroic.
This is not a full memory list but
a brainstorm for the future meeting on
what you were today, and on what to feel,

subsequently. When you saw me reading
Lewis & Clark, you said, "I just read that."
And you did, ten years ago in a boxcar,
just a moment ago, before I looked

at you, when you were dreaming in the moss-
dampened daylight of Jimmie Walker swamp.

Kaos

With your son Cary's *Kaos* tagged on the backboard,
Dave shot hoops in the rain, aiming for net
and a denting bounce on the orange
Rabbit's hood. You took that VW piece of shit

off the hands of your retired colleague. I wonder why?
You already had three equally unreliable
squirrel squats, raccoon crack houses, parked in the mudway.
I think you piled these cars not only for yourself

but for your friends, imagining each of us
shedding hubcaps in your peripheral vision or
rear-view mirror, as you coasted to Cape Hatteras
completely alone. Having given us each our own

rusted coffin, you have us broken down in rain-beaded
glass, admiring your fancy-smooth ride to lucky numbers.

Strudels

I was going to bring Schwartz's smoked meat,
St. Viateur bagels and chocolate cream pie
from Laurier BBQ. But rain beat down
as I drove up St. Lawrence Street.

I was kidding myself, I couldn't get all this
alone and still be in bed by midnight. I went
to Cantor's and bought chocolate Danish,
apple turnovers, two apple strudels,

and then to Metro grocery store, where
I picked up bite sized brownies, tiny sugar-
covered doughnuts, two Swiss chocolate bars
(one with hazelnuts), two onions (one red,

one white), ground beef (lean), Paris mushrooms,
with the idea that I could make spaghetti sauce.

Hutchison

When I lived with you that summer on Hutchison,
I remember you going about your business one
afternoon, cooking meat sauce in a cast-iron
pan. I'd never seen a man cook before (except

the odd smoked meat mish-mash my father made).
You put oil, onions and garlic in first, then
browned the ground beef. I remember thinking,
"So that's the meat in meat sauce." It was so simple.

You cooked the sauce at your leisure, humming
country tunes to the TV news, pondering
lines from history books, the world left simmering.
I don't remember you eating it, but you probably

ate it in front of CNN, relishing the flavour
like a good smoke after finishing something of a poem.

Sonnet of the Bars

When we try to reach beyond the bars,
we find we can only reach between them.
That's how I feel about the way you held
my hand in your hand for a while longer

even though we knew I was not supposed
to be helping you up, that I could not
pull you through this impossible surprise
of reaching arms. No helping you up, no

pulling you through, but a warm grasp
justified by gestures to help you up,
pull you through my pretend bars
all made of arms that pulse and themselves reach

beyond the frame of this jail of reaching arms.
Can't risk jailbreak for fear of harming delicate warm arms.

Summer Caravan

It's not jealousy of what you might feel
for others in the room, it's just the need
to feel myself alive in puppet play—
and please, not faintly alive. Professor

(i.e. head puppeteer), who am I to be in your
Punch & Judy show? Please, some sidekick to your
Punch, a low-level fractal, chaos apprentice,
baby-devil Ketch-killer. Sausages! Let me

be your sausages! Wind me 'round death's
neck and play a trick, cry raspy jibes through
your swazzle reeds, sting life with your stick.
Watch yourself watch yourself from the seaside

fit-up. You're screaming, "That's the way to do
it!" Please, Professor, let me get a laugh.

Adiós Sonnet

When I said goodbye, I made sure to look
you in the eye and tell you I'd be back soon.
You said okay, and then a few seconds later,
my back already turned to you, I heard

you call out, *Adios*. I thought it funny
and casual, at first, like a cute *adios amigos*
thing, but then I started thinking, isn't
that just the same as saying "Adieu"

but in Spanish, and doesn't that mean
"To God," as in, *That's where I'm going.
See you there*? We're mounted on our horses.
You will head west through Kansas, Nebraska,

Wyoming, etc., eat strange animals on the Oregon Trail,
I'll drive my Subaru back to Montreal.

Trilby

It rained thoroughly all the way back. Dave
and Jon wanted to stop at Burger King
(our favourite meal on the way home from
golf with you at Dufferin Heights), but I

just wanted to be in the car alone.
I dropped them off without fanfare—Dave was
off to NYC, Jon needed to move
your Land Rover or else get a ticket—

and parked on Hutchison for just a while.
You were dating Trilby when we lived here.
I hadn't read the novel yet, didn't
know your Trilby looked exactly like George

Du Maurier's statuesque heroine,
or that you were a true bohemian.

Les Méchants Mardis

They went to sleep without any fuss at all. Oscar
(age 4) climbed into his bed and covered himself.
Good night. Nava (age 3) didn't even want a story,
just a song and a kiss. They knew I needed them

away. What for? So I could stare at the Habs lose
to the Blackhawks 2-1. So I could look at all
your books on my poetry shelf. So I could read
a passage from *Napoleon's Retreat,* two poems

from *Ricky Ricardo Suites*. So I could compare
the inscription you wrote in *Standing Wave*
to the one you wrote me in *The Encantadas*
at the last reading we did together, Boa Bar,

September 16th, 2006. So I could finally
realize you figured me in the past tense.

Inscriptions

Here is how you signed my copy of *The Encantadas:*
"For Jason, my friend, fellow poet and golfing
buddy. Thanks for everything you've done
and meant. Love, Rob 9/16/06."

At the time, I focused on the word *meant*
in a paranoid way, thinking it might mean
"everything you've done, and have meant
to do"—referring to ways in which I've

failed you. I couldn't think of any offhand,
but was certain there must have been examples
that you remembered. But now it reads more
clearly as a message, an admission: "everything

you have done and have meant to me."
Neither sense is in the least consoling.

Sonnet of A to H

Alvin has done. Archie has meant. Astaire has
been to the top of the stairs. Athena has forgotten
Botticelli's papers at the bottom of the stairs.
Bloom has returned to the bottom of the stairs to retrieve

Buddy Ebsen's papers. Captain Beefheart
has kissed Columbus's children good night. Davy Crockett
has kissed Daphne's daughter Darwin good night. Derrida
has kissed his wife Dionysus goodbye. Elly May

has kissed Elvis's children goodbye. Ethel has written
a few things. Franklin has spoken about
meaningful things to Frye. Galapagos Ted
has loved Gertrude Stein very deeply, Gilligan

very deeply, Ginger very deeply. Homer Simpson
has meant something to a few certain people.

Sonnet of J to Z

Jack has done. Jesus has meant. John Deere has
been to the top of the stairs. Johnny Cash has forgotten
Keith Richards's papers at the bottom of the stairs.
Mia has returned to the bottom of the stairs

to retrieve Mick Jagger's papers. Montaigne
has kissed Moses's children good night. Nabokov
has kissed Odysseus's daughter Olive Oyl good night.
Orpheus has kissed his wife Oz goodbye. Plato

has kissed Popeye's children goodbye. Rubens
has written Sinatra. Skipper has spoken about
Swee'Pea to Thucydides. Tom Waits
has loved Scheherazade very deeply, Telemachus

very deeply, Woody very deeply. Zappa
has meant something to Zeus.

Showdown

Kit Schubert versus the Peacock Angel:
Both are conceptual, PA conceived
of feather and flesh, KS conceived of
wax and nerve and bone. Neither is good

and that's what makes each one so appealing.
PA sees porn in the dust wakes of bright ghosts,
KS humped wax effigies of Snow White.
Their favourite dwarves were Grumpy, Sneezy,

and especially the ones that got cut:
Horny, Scabby, Jealousy, Sadistic Mo Fo.
When Kit and Peacock hung out together,
it was a bad scene bound to end in pain.

Their jump in unison from the knife's edge
made quills to write a satire sealed with wax.

News

Anne took the red-eye to Toronto from Vancouver
so she could help Vivienne drive you back
to Ayer's Cliff. With the pain in your legs
it took them nine hours to make that trip,

and it drained you so that you could walk
before you left, and hardly sit up by yourself
when you arrived. Mikhail knew all this
when I picked him up Sunday morning

on Villeneuve Street. He was sullen
and hungover from entertaining Russians
the night before. That Russian gathering was planned
before he heard you were very sick. He drank

vodka until it was finished, and then
wine because there was no vodka left.

Sonnet after Daniil Kharms

To drive—to fly—to walk. And now the car drove.
And now the nail drove. And now the news drove.
And now the lunacy. And now the plane flew.
And now the lark flew. The swallows. The owl. The dove.

And now the hat flew. And now time. And now time
too quickly. And now a thought flies. An eye
flies. And now a fly flies. And thoughts, too quickly.
And then a fleeting dream. It flies too, of course.

And now a boy walks. And now a batter walks.
And now a dainty fawn walks for the first time.
And now a man walks. And a fancy speed walker.
And now a man with a cane. And now a priest,

a rabbi and an Irish policeman walk into
a bar. And now wet yellow leaves fly by.

Sunday

We picked up bagels at St. Viateur and made
good time to Ayer's Cliff. I can't remember a single
thing we talked about until Steve arrived
at about eleven. Steve brought you the *New York*

Times and you read the sports page front
to back as we sat in chairs near your bed
talking publishing, Afghanistan, the World
Series, trains, global oil producers, etc. Misha told

the story about Roman "The Purse" Abramovich—
how he was holding all of Putin's money,
but now his supermodel divorcee
might get Putin's assets in the divorce

settlement. A bullet in the head is what
she'll get. You read the paper thoroughly.

Times

This is just what you would have done
on any regular Sunday. Anne leaned over
and said something like, *Rob, remember
how I used to get upset because you read*

your paper instead of talking to me?
Todd had told me a similar story.
In Marylebone, he brought you
to his favorite diner, the one the Kinks

used to haunt. You settled into your paper
for two hours without saying a word.
I had to reassure Todd that he actually
had shared time with you. You need to read

the paper. Your appetite for news is voracious.
You are autonomous, content, and often quiet.

Satellite Sonnet

You read all of the baseball news, and spent
a long time on the stats. Steve told the story
of how you would study for high school math
with two radios on, turning from your text-

book to the two game-logs you were keeping.
Your love to hear games called. Last May
you showed me your XM Satellite Radio
receiver, boasting that now you could

hear any game, no matter where you were.
Perfect for hearing your Dodgers as you
coasted through Virginia. As Steve left
he said, *Enjoy your pristine Sunday NY Times.*

But from behind newsprint, you called him out:
This paper was read before it got here!

Fable

"The Tortoise and the Hare." There once was
a lazy Tortoise, slow and fat, but
smooth with the ladies. He liked to take
them inside and spend cozy times there

in front of the fire, telling them all the same
story about the Hare. Sometimes the Hare
would come by in person with an empty
sugar jar, knock on the Tortoise's shell

and yell, *Tortoise, I need some sugar,
please!* Tortoise would stick a leg out
and hand the Hare a tin can full of white
"sugar." But when the Hare added Tortoise's

sugar to his coffee, he found it would bubble
and fizz. *Baking soda again!* exclaimed the Hare.

Petersburg

Misha brought me to St. Petersburg last
summer. You were meant to come, too. We would
have hung out at the Duty Free. Pictures
I would have taken: Rob in jean shirt between

Bank Bridge gold-winged griffons. Rob in fancy
cowboy shirt next to Egyptian Bridge gold-
tiara'd sphinx. Rob holding black can of
Baltika (beer) between white lions on

the Lion Bridge. The Pavel Sokolov/
Robert Allen bridge series, I would have
written in my little Petersburg album.
I would have shown you off to my "baby

Russian" friends, Brooklynites who left Russia
at age six and now translate Daniil Kharms.

Atwater Market

It is difficult to know what is worth
mentioning because it means drawing
you out from inside your quiet theatre.
I told you that I'd taken Oscar and

Nava to Atwater market for pumpkins.
Oscar chose a big one, Nava a small one.
In my kitchen, we drew triangle eyes and
nose, and a big gaping smile on Oscar's

pumpkin, and they were fascinated
as I cut the face out with a wide
kitchen knife. When I uncapped the top,
Oscar was afraid to reach his hand inside

the pumpkin's head. You would have had
a funny song to dispel his pumpkin fear.

Sonnet of the 7th Moon

It's the end of October, time for the
Seventh Moon. This same month, 1975,
you read with Ralph Gustafson, D. G.
Jones, Claudia Lapp, Michael Oliver,

Avrum Malus, Réal Faucher, and Michael
Harris at Le Moulin Coffee House in
North Hatley, "The Legend of 'Creepy Fingers'
Karpis." A poem about Alvin, Public

Enemy Number 1, released from the U.S.
to end his days on Rue Doloreuse
in Montreal. Long-haired, leather-jacketed
and mustached—smiling, and happy, I think—

the last line you read that night portrayed Alvin
asleep, as "a gold-eyed duffle of dreams."

Owls

With these visits I feel like the winter sparrow,
in one window out the other, back into the storm.
A warmth briefly given when I get to sit
near you on the floor, and just stare

at you, or the floor, or your collection
of Anne's owls perched on a corner shelf
above you. Are these ceramic owls
the husks of that memory of the snowy

owl you trapped with your father
on December 15th, 1963? Archie
the owl, you named him, kept him
alive, with your father, together, by feeding

him sparrows whole, watching his eyes darken
as he gave the little birds interminable warmth.

At the OK

At night we return to Valhalla to feast
on roasted boar and drink dark mead.
Those who don't go home wind up in hell
or any number of other places that are not Valhalla.

And even Valhalla can be any number of places.
Mine is not the same as yours. Mine is someplace
in the future, where chair technology is so advanced
one feels nothing when one sits. Where people

don't lean but float while they wait. And the mead,
oh, its special "future mead," like liquid manna, with a very
pleasing fizz. Through the back slats of your Valhalla,
you can watch Doc Holliday, Morgan Earp, go to town.

Your mead tastes better sitting on Arizona wood chairs,
with gunfire at the OK Corral, blasting daily at 2 p.m.

Epigram

I think you are nicer than Theodore
Dreiser, cuter than Matthew Zapruder,
more daft than Sylvia Plath, have more chops
than Elizabeth Bishop, and you wear

despair better than Charles Baudelaire.
You're more apropos than Edgar Poe, and
you poetically examine better
than A. R. Ammons. You can chase a thrill

longer than Herman Melville, you deal with
love more elegantly than Nabokov,
walk into a casino with more Tarantino
than Gilbert Sorrentino. More bitchin'

than Pynchon, more like a child than Oscar Wilde,
you knew what you wanted more than Dante did.

After Antigone

I wonder what bird you're speaking to now.
A bird that sees you with both eyes at once
and acknowledges what others fail to.
Are you grasping it firmly in both hands,

a feathered heart that must be held that way?
Or are you guarding it as it paces
your writing desk and records random things
with gentle talons? Meanwhile, the poets

back in the bar roll their own little birds
from their tongues. The dirty little birds loop
like blotto swallows among smoke rings still
deforming from years ago, among decaying

voices that said better things, dispersing
atoms breathed by people who mattered once.

Lines for a White Cat

Lines for a black and white dog: You were
Cory's, not mine, and I think she felt you held
a best part of herself. When Oscar was born, you slept
at the foot of his crib, on guard, even though

you understood he meant the end of Cory's best
attention. We had an appointment to put you down
in two days. But when you could no longer walk,
you decided to leave on your own terms.

I worked at home that day, and you lay on a
Mexican blanket at my feet, with towels
when needed. At night I carried you to your
spot on the floor, next to our bed. You listened,

ears up, to the kids as we put them to sleep. Sometime
(around 8 p.m.) when their voices were quiet, you died.

Variation on "Making It"

Variation on an early poem of Rob's:
Tortoise thinks the aim of gardens should be
making table and shithouse for Toity
(Grandview Teddy, last of a dying breed),

making him shade in the late afternoon.
But they all have their shade, from the deep blue
dragonfly, to brown Irene hoping to
be captured in a not-taken photo.

Gardens are for going into, coming
out of, though for Grandview Teddy
it's half his life to trelliswork walking,
no time to spend with friendly escapees,

if he wants a spot in the family plot.
A garden's aim: to survive cold to hot.

Sonnet after Valéry

The Lost Wine (after Valéry): Once I
(but I can't recall under what heavens)
threw, as an offering to the abyss,
a little bit of precious evening wine.

Who wanted you to spill, O alcohol?
Was I moved by some divine being, perhaps?
Or maybe some deep worry in my heart,
some dream of blood, moved me to spill you, wine?

Its gauzy costume, like a frosted rose,
dissolved into the ocean's purity.
Hardly a tint remained upon the sea.
Lost, this wine, to the lucky drunken waves.

I have since seen floating in bitter air
the foggiest figures of my despair.

Sonnet after Verlaine

After Verlaine: There is crying in my heart
as there is rain on the city. What is
this exhaustion that penetrates my heart?
O for the soft din of the rain

soaking the ground, striking the roofs!
For a heart that's jammed like a coin-op TV
there is nothing so soothing, consoling,
as the dreadful marimba-playing of the rain.

The pointless song of the rain! It spreads without
reason in the chambers of my vacant heart.
This is the worst kind of boring sorrow,
to be fixed in plastic seat before the tube,

to know the reception will not improve,
to feel deep sadness, but not hate, not love.

Sonnet after Baudelaire

Tough Luck (after Baudelaire): To push off
a boulder that big and heavy, Mr. Sisyphus,
would take truly Sisyphusian cojones!
Even though your heart may be in it,

art is interminable, life terminal.
Away from the famous sepulchers,
on the road to a solitary cemetery,
my heart, like a tautened caul-drum,

pounds out a brutal funeral march.
Countless jewels sleep alone in crypts
of darkness and forgetting, far from the hands
of gravediggers and gothic teenage vandals.

Have you any idea how many
flowers exhale perfume for nobody?

House Party

Against all evidence, I expect to find you upright,
fixing the fire, empty scotch glass on floor,
book splayed words-down on love seat, when
I step into the cabin tomorrow morning.

I expect some girls, smart ones, and pretty,
sitting in a circle, talking. Plus former students,
present ones and old friends. I expect weed, bad wine
and everything to be calm and sweet as always.

I expect it to be nighttime, with stars, a bonfire,
midnight basketball, a sing-song, a joke-telling
contest, riddles, ghost stories, and giddy mimicry,
some personal opinions, not gossip, just confessions.

A party going on for you long after
you are asleep on all our piled-up coats.

Advice on Angry Mourning

Advice on angry mourning from the Fall
lyric generator: See what flows from your
mushy pen. Purchase some flabby wings for
hovering. Piss off Jesus in a bar.

Go delirious for eight seconds a day.
At 10:35, play "Send in the Clowns."
Act ten times your height, one-tenth your age.
Make a career of what you're doing now.

Drop out, become a no-man, live your rules.
Smell vegetarians, but don't eat them.
Positively derange curious fools.
Cultivate your speech impediment.

Dress like a road beacon, but don't try to be free.
Drink a jar of coffee. Take a jar of these....

Road Trip

The last trip to the cabin was at night.
I picked Jon up at school around 6 p.m.
We drove through rain and listened to punk rock.
Arrived at 8 with wine and vulgar hope.

Idea was to listen to baseball.
Game 3 of the 2006 World Series.
Your XM radio couldn't pick it up.
The Cardinals beat the Tigers five to zip.

But we had no idea as we talked.
We read through all of your old golf scorecards.
Records of days spent on the Stanstead hills.
Defeating faithful Steve with your short game.

You listened and observed 'til past midnight.
Watching from the tenth tee of Dufferin Heights.

Write, Drink, Sleep, Dream

Write, drink, sleep, dream, polite eye-blink wink gleam,
white zinc sheep cream, ignite fire-pink rubbish-
heap laser beam, alight brink-steep sorrow-
seam, bright ink weep team, recite in-sync bleep

theme, water-sprite ice-rink sweep team, leaf-blight
cinquefoil creep scheme, burial-site clink-
clink reap scream, recite think-peep theme, tightly
interlinked weep machine, quite a stinking

weep stream, night think weep extreme,
tooth-bite black-mink deep careen, warning-light
blinking jeep high-beams, black-kite trinket keep
redeem, all-night drink-cheap carpe diem,

overwrite shrinking weep meme, speed-of-light
tinkling leap balance-beam, *write, drink, sleep, dream.*

Aube Lumière

In your hospice room, objects sleep soundly,
without the dread of loss. Shoes sleep on the floor
and a closed book reads itself to sleep, but becomes
too engrossed. There are two cups and two saucers,

chipped and asleep now and silent beside
one tarnished spoon reflecting nothing,
dry in its scoop. Metal sleep, ceramic sleep,
paper sleep. Bagels sleep stacked in a brown

paper bag and don't dare stir or rustle in the
bag. Bread sleep. One-hundred-percent-natural
cranberry juice sleeps in a small glass and a drinking
straw sleeps half-immersed in red liquid,

which, when asleep, looks like Jell-O, solid red.
If objects dream, it's without sense of distance or remorse.

Cliff House Blues

Close the doors, pull down the blinds,
turn the record player off,
put the books back on the shelves,
wash the last few dishes in the sink.

Spill out the whiskey and the wine,
fold up the sheets, wash the floors,
burn the chairs, fill the woodstove
with cement, put the guitar back in

its case, unplug the lights and the TV,
wrap the trip log in steel bands,
remove the pictures from the walls,
lock all the little things in drawers.

Welcome the rain, grab hold the dirt.
put your hands upon your head.

I am writing just because I can

I write because I miss knowing you're here.
I miss your wisdom and debauchery—
the way you liked to redraw the frontier
to suit your purpose, or just to be contrary.

I write because I don't know you're not here.
I know it, sure, but I don't really know
what I know. I expect you to appear
at the threshold of a tabagie in the plateau

and explain what it means that you're not here.
Explain your protest against the heat death
of your universe, explain in severe
terms the flavours of the waters of Lethe.

I write because some things can't be buried.
I miss your wisdom and debauchery.

Acknowledgments

Earlier versions of some poems in this collection have appeared previously in *Jacket*, *London Magazine*, *The New Quarterly*, *Matrix*, and *Babylon Burning: 9/11 Five Years On, Poems in Aid of the Red Cross*.

Many people have read and responded to versions of these poems as they were being written. My warm gratitude to Jon Paul Fiorentino, Judith Herz, Mikhail Iossel, Steve Luxton and Anne Stone.

Thanks to Todd Swift and Alessandro Porco for sharing their thoughts on the poems. Very special thanks to David McGimpsey for getting me to write this book, and for some crucial, Skyped comments at the very end.

Thanks to Mike O'Connor, Dan Varrette, Insomniac Press, and to my editor, Paul Vermeersch, for his support of this manuscript and the insightful comments he made upon it.

The voice of Robert Allen was in my ear throughout the writing of this book, and I am thankful for his continued influence even in his absence.

Most important: Cory, Oscar, Nava.